To: ....

From: ....

date: ....

Eleanor
the Hippo

Learns to Tell
the Truth

Text and Art by
Andy McGuire

HARVEST HOUSE PUBLISHERS

EUGENE, OREGON

Books & Such Literary Agency
52 Mission Circle, Suite 122, PMB 170
Santa Rosa, CA 95409-5370
www.booksandsuch.biz

ELEANOR THE HIPPO LEARNS TO
TELL THE TRUTH
Text and art copyright © 2011 by Andy McGuire
Published by Harvest House Publishers
Eugene, Oregon 97402
www.harvesthousepublishers.com

ISBN 978-0-7369-2665-2

Design and production by Franke Design and Illustration, Minneapolis, Minnesota

Printed in China

11 12 13 14 15 16 17 / LP / 10 9 8 7 6 5 4 3 2 1

Eleanor hippo talked a lot,
Which is good sometimes...
But sometimes not.

It's fine to have a conversation
Full of honest information,
But sadly what she'd sometimes do
Is tell a tale that wasn't true.

She thought that she was having fun,
But lies can often hurt someone.

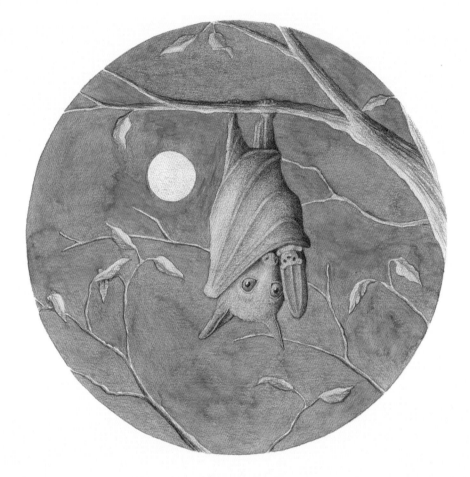

She'd say, "You know that bat named Clark?
Can you believe he's afraid of the dark?

And I heard that silly frog named Fred
Turned eight, but he *still* wets the bed!"

It was nonstop fibbing night and day;
You never could tell what she might say.

Her mama said, "Eleanor, you'll regret it."
But Eleanor never seemed to get it—
Her life seemed good, so why upset it?

One day Eleanor sat around
With zebras who were new in town.

She made up stuff that wasn't true,
Of crazy things the locals do.

She told on every beast and bird;
The crowd was loving every word.
But then she did a foolish thing—
She lied about the local king!

"**O**ur lion is a scaredy-cat,
He's terrified of this and that.
A friend heard Leo yelping when
He found a spider in his den."

The crowd all gasped—for zebras know
That even if this tale were so

You just don't mock a lion's flaws—
It's breaking all the jungle's laws,
And lions have all those teeth and claws!

Late that night as Eleanor snored
Across the river, something roared!

Could that have been a sound of warning?
Or would it all clear up by morning?
But pretty soon a mean hyena
Said, "Eleanor, Leo wants to see ya!"

With that, the strangest thing occurred—
Eleanor couldn't say a word.

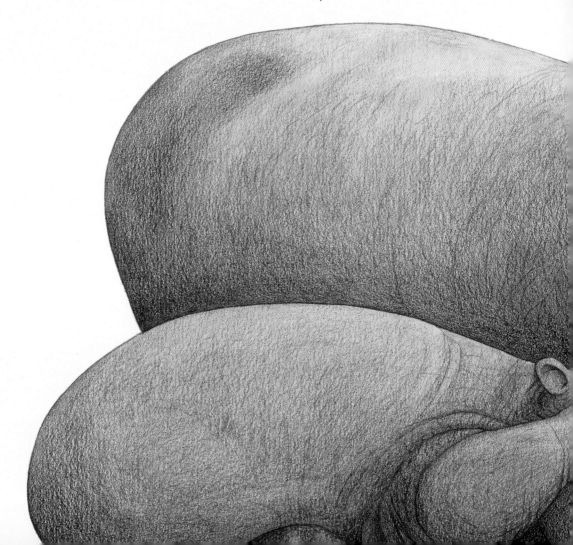

Her mama looked her in the eyes
And whispered, "Just apologize."

So off she went on trembly knees
Working through some strategies.

She hadn't finished thinking when
she found herself outside his den.

Poor Eleanor stood there terrified
Until, at last, she walked inside.

But what she saw was mystifying—

Leo's eyes were red from crying.

23

"You hurt my feelings, Eleanor,
And no one fears me anymore.
Your lying was the end of me—
An honest-to-goodness catastrophe!"

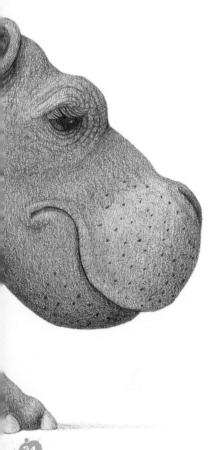

Then just like that guess what appeared?
The spider Leo supposedly feared.
Well, he stayed calm just as before.

The one who screamed was Eleanor.

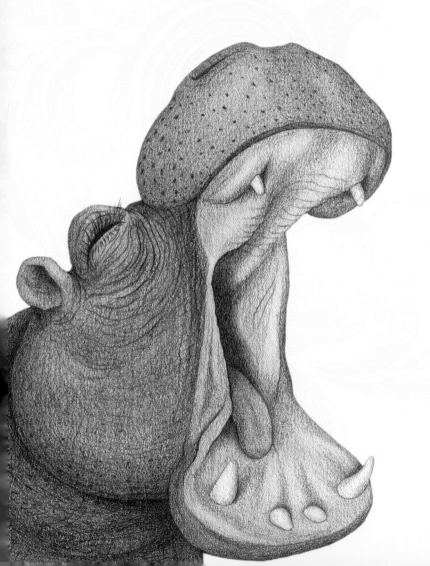

She ran out yelling, "Help! A spider!"
Then noticed all her friends beside her.
The crowd now clearly understood—
She'd fibbed to make herself look good.

The truth had overcome the lies,
Which shouldn't be a big surprise.
Since truth is strong and fibs are weak,
Eventually all lies spring a leak.

"I'm sorry," whispered Eleanor.
"I won't be lying anymore."

That day she learned a thing or two.
Now what she says is always true.

No claiming that the leopard steals,

Exaggerating python meals,

Or saying that the mean hyena
Dances like a ballerina.

The honest truth, many say,
Is more surprising anyway!